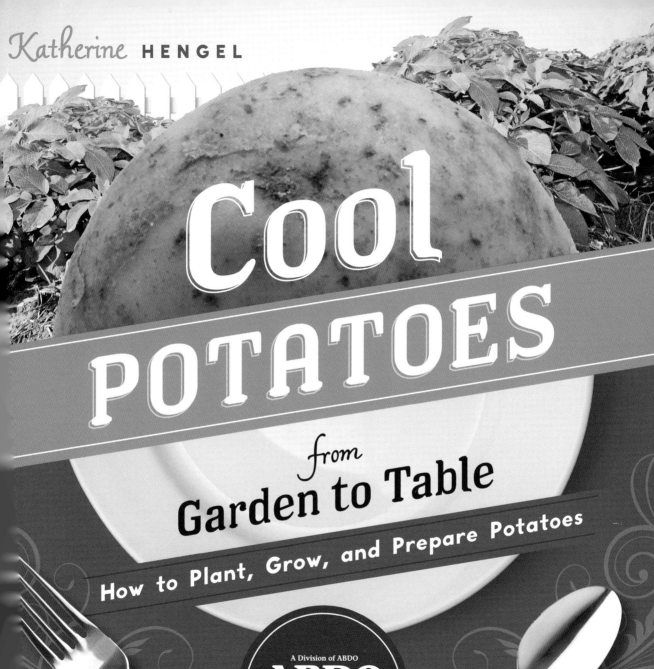

Katherine HENGEL

Cool
POTATOES

from
Garden to Table

How to Plant, Grow, and Prepare Potatoes

A Division of ABDO
ABDO
Publishing Company

visit us at www.abdopublishing.com

Published by ABDO Publishing Company, a division of ABDO, P.O. Box 398166, Minneapolis, Minnesota 55439. Copyright © 2012 by Abdo Consulting Group, Inc. International copyrights reserved in all countries. No part of this book may be reproduced in any form without written permission from the publisher. Checkerboard Library™ is a trademark and logo of ABDO Publishing Company.

Printed in the United States of America, North Mankato, Minnesota
102011
012012

 PRINTED ON RECYCLED PAPER

Design and Production: Anders Hanson, Mighty Media, Inc.
Series Editor: Liz Salzmann
Photo Credits: Aaron DeYoe, Shutterstock. Photos on page 5 courtesy of W. Atlee Burpee & Co.

The following manufacturers/names appearing in this book are trademarks: Hormel™, Pam®, Gold Medal Flour®, Hellmann's®, Market Pantry®, Crystal Sugar®, Pyrex®, Kitchen Aid®

Library of Congress Cataloging-in-Publication Data
Hengel, Katherine.
  Cool potatoes from garden to table : how to plant, grow, and prepare potatoes / Katherine Hengel.
    p. cm. -- (Cool garden to table)
  Includes index.
  ISBN 978-1-61783-186-7
  1. Potatoes--Juvenile literature. 2. Cooking (Potatoes)--Juvenile literature. I. Title.
  SB211.P8H46 2012
  635'.21--dc23
                    2011037249

Safety First!

Some recipes call for activities or ingredients that require caution. If you see these symbols, ask an adult for help!

Sharp - You need to use a sharp knife or cutting tool for this recipe.

Hot - This recipe requires handling hot objects. Always use oven mitts when holding hot pans.

CONTENTS

WHY GROW YOUR OWN FOOD?

Because then you get to eat it, of course! You might not be the biggest potato fan in the world. But have you ever had fresh potatoes? Straight from your very own garden? If not, prepare to be surprised. Fresh food tastes wonderful!

Plus, fresh food is really healthy. All produce is good for you. But produce that comes from your own garden is the very best. Most folks do not use chemicals in their home gardens. That makes home gardens better for you and the **environment**!

Growing your own food is rewarding. All it takes is time, patience, soil, water, and sunshine! This book will teach you how to grow potatoes in **containers**. Once they're ready, you can use them in some tasty recipes!

ALL ABOUT
POTATOES

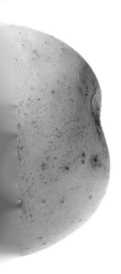

Potatoes are one of the world's main food crops. It's easy to see why! You can grow a lot of potatoes with less work than many other foods. They also adapt well to different climates. They grow and can be stored underground!

There are more than 5,000 kinds of potatoes. Each looks, tastes, and grows differently! In this book, we're going to grow and cook Yukon Golds. Yukon Golds are a kind of yellow potato, and they grow very well in **containers**. Let's get started!

TYPES OF POTATOES

RUSSIAN BANANA

ROSE FIN APPLE

YUKON GOLD

DAISY GOLD

GROWING

In this book, you'll learn how to grow potatoes in a **container** garden. With container gardens, you have more control over things such as light and temperature. But keep in mind that potatoes grow differently in every climate.

When to Plant

Go online to find out the average date of the last frost in your area. Plant your seed potatoes about two weeks before this date.

The Right Conditions

Sunlight
Potato plants need six to eight hours of sunlight a day.

Temperature
*Potato plants will not grow until the soil temperature has reached 45 **degrees**. They grow best between 60 and 70 degrees.*

The Right Soil
Potatoes take a lot of nutrients from the soil. They need fertile, loose, well-draining loam.

SOW YOUR SEEDS

1

2

3

MATERIALS NEEDED

5-gallon container with drainage holes

potting soil mix

2-inch-wide, certified-organic seed potato, sprouted

water

trowel

(1) Fill the **container** one-third full of soil. Put the seed potato on top. Add just enough soil to cover it. Water it immediately.

(2) When the plant is about 6 inches (15 cm) tall, add a hill of soil around the plant. The hill should be 2 to 3 inches (5 to 7 cm) high.

(3) Every time the plant grows 6 inches (15 cm) taller than the soil, add another hill. This is called *hilling*.

4 Continue hilling until the soil is about 1 to 2 inches (2.5 to 5 cm) from the top of the container.

STAGES OF

Watering

The soil should be evenly moist, but not too wet. Always water your plants in the morning. Stop watering the potato plant when the leaves turn yellow.

Hilling

Hilling is when you add more soil around the plant. The new potatoes grow above the original seed potato. That's why hilling is important. Use **compost** whenever you can.

WATER the plant in the morning. Keep the soil evenly moist.

HILL the plant again each time there are 6 inches (15 cm) showing above the soil.

HILL the plant when it is 6 inches (15 cm) tall.

FERTILIZE once a month. Add water soluble fertilizer when you water the plant.

GROWTH

Fertilizing

Find a high-quality **fertilizer** that is water **soluble**. Use it once a month when you water your plant. Your potato plant will love you.

Harvesting

Most potato plants live for about four months above ground. Then they begin to wilt. When the leaves turn brown and die, the potatoes are **mature** and ready to eat!

Don't WATER after the leaves turn yellow.

HARVEST the potatoes when the plant grows flowers and the leaves turn brown.

HARVESTING

POTATOES

(1) Before harvesting, get the soil around the potatoes very wet.

(2) Use a shovel or garden fork to help dig the potatoes out of the soil. Be careful not to **damage** them!

(3) Before using the potatoes, **scrub** them with a vegetable brush. Rinse them in cold water.

4 Store potatoes in a dark, cool place. The ideal storage temperature is about 40 **degrees**.

How long will it take?

It depends on the sun, temperature and type of potato. Most potatoes are ready in 70 to 90 days.

Why are there black spots in the middle of my potatoes?

Black or hollow centers are caused by over-watering. When you water, the soil should be thoroughly wet. But don't let it become **waterlogged**.

Why are my potatoes shaped funny?

Not watering often enough can cause the potatoes to have bumps.

Why are there black spots on the leaves of my potato plant?

Potato **blight** attacks the leaves first. Then the potatoes. If your leaves have black spots, cut down the plant. Leave just 2 inches (5 cm) of stem above the soil. This results in a smaller harvest, but at least you'll get a few potatoes!

Cool Ingredients

BACON BITS

BUTTER

CAYENNE PEPPER

CHEDDAR CHEESE

NON-STICK COOKING SPRAY

CANNED CORN

DICED HAM

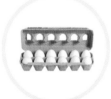
EGGS

FLOUR

GREEN ONIONS

MAYONNAISE

MILK

*Some people are **allergic** to certain foods. This means they can get very sick if they eat them. They might need **emergency** medical help. Nut allergies are serious and can be especially harmful. Before you serve anything made with nuts or peanut oil, ask if anyone has a nut allergy.*

OLIVE OIL

ONION

ONION SOUP MIX

PARSLEY FLAKES

PEPPER

SALT

SOUR CREAM

SUGAR

THYME

VEGETABLE OIL

Kitchen Tools

ALUMINUM FOIL

BAKING SHEET

CUTTING BOARD

FORK

GRATER

LARGE POT

MEASURING CUPS

MEASURING SPOONS

MEDIUM POT

MIXING BOWLS

MIXING SPOON

NON-STICK
FRYING PAN

SHREDDING CHEESE AT HOME

You can shred or grate cheese yourself using a grater! Of course, you can buy prepared cheese in packages too. This saves some time in the kitchen. But it's usually a bit more expensive than doing it yourself.

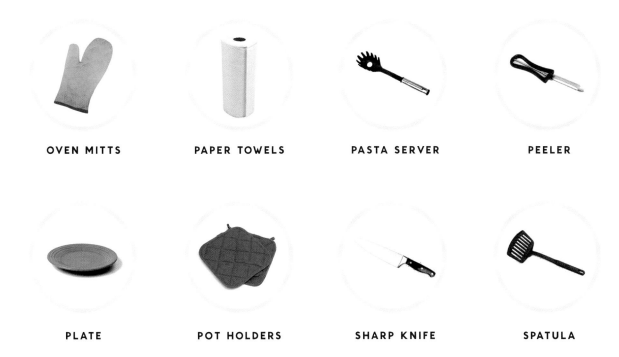

OVEN MITTS   **PAPER TOWELS**   **PASTA SERVER**   **PEELER**

PLATE   **POT HOLDERS**   **SHARP KNIFE**   **SPATULA**

SPOON   **STRAINER**

Cooking Terms

Arrange

Arrange means to place things in a certain order or pattern.

Boil

Boil means to heat liquid until it begins to bubble.

Coat

Coat means to cover something with another ingredient or mixture.

Chop

Chop means to cut into small pieces.

Dice

Dice means to cut something into small squares with a knife.

Mash

Mash means to press down and smash food with a fork or potato masher.

Peel

Peel means to remove the skin, often with a peeler.

Toss

Toss means to turn ingredients over to coat them with seasonings.

LENGTHWISE OR CROSSWISE

To cut something lengthwise means to cut along its length. You create pieces that are the same length as the original.

To cut something crosswise means to cut across its length. The pieces will be shorter, but the same width as the original.

OH, YEAH!

Oven Fries

A simple and tasty way to enjoy potatoes!

MAKES 6 SERVINGS

18

INGREDIENTS

non-stick
cooking spray

2½ pounds
yellow potatoes

1 teaspoon
vegetable oil

1 tablespoon sugar

1 teaspoon salt

cayenne pepper

TOOLS

baking sheet

aluminum foil

cutting board

sharp knife

mixing bowl

measuring spoons

pasta server

oven mitts

1   Preheat the oven to 450 **degrees**. Line a baking sheet with aluminum foil. Coat the foil with non-stick cooking spray.

2   Wash and **scrub** the potatoes. Cut each potato in half lengthwise.

③   Place a potato half flat-side down on the cutting board. Cut it lengthwise into ½-inch (1 cm) strips.

④   Remove the two end strips. Turn the sliced potato half on its side. Stack the strips evenly. Cut the stack lengthwise into ½-inch (1 cm) strips.

5   Repeat steps 3 and 4 for each potato half.

⑥   Put the potato strips in a large bowl. Add the oil, sugar, salt, and a **pinch** of cayenne pepper. Toss to coat the potatoes.

⑦   Put the potatoes on the baking sheet in an even layer. Bake for 30 minutes, or until potatoes are tender and browned.

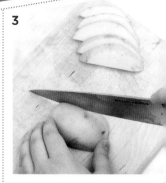

3

4

6

7

POSITIVELY
Potato Soup

This creamy soup is sure to please!

MAKES 6 TO 8 SERVING

INGREDIENTS

6 yellow
potatoes, peeled

1 onion

½ cup butter, cut
into chunks

½ cup flour

1 cup diced,
cooked ham

1 teaspoon
parsley flakes

2 cups milk

salt and pepper

TOOLS

large pot

cutting board

sharp knife

strainer

large bowl

pot holders

mixing spoon

measuring cups

measuring spoons

1. Boil a large pot of water. While it is heating up, chop the potatoes and onion. Add both to the boiling water. Cook for about 10 minutes, or until potatoes are tender.

2. Hold or set a strainer over a large bowl. Ask an adult to help carefully empty the pot into the strainer. Measure 4 cups of the potato water. Set it aside.

3. Put the potatoes and onions back in the pot. Turn the heat to low. Add the butter. Stir until the butter is melted

4. Add the flour, ham, and parsley. Stir lightly. Add the milk and potato water. Turn the heat up to medium. Stir until the soup thickens. This takes about 5 minutes. Add salt and pepper to taste.

5. Put the soup in serving bowls. **Garnish** each bowl with a few leaves of parsley.

1

3

4

TEMPTING
Twice-Baked Potatoes

These tasty spuds can be an appetizer or main dish!

MAKES 4 SERVINGS

INGREDIENTS

2 yellow potatoes

¼ cup grated cheddar cheese

2 tablespoons butter

2 tablespoons milk

2 tablespoons chopped onion

salt and pepper

1 tablespoon chopped green onions

TOOLS

fork

oven mitts

spoon

mixing bowl

grater

measuring cups

measuring spoons

cutting board

sharp knife

baking sheet

1

(1) Preheat the oven to 400 **degrees**. Poke each potato several times with a fork. Bake the potatoes in the preheated oven for 45 minutes. To see if they are done, stick a fork in one. The fork should enter easily.

2

(2) Once the potatoes are done, remove them from the oven. Let the potatoes cool slightly. Cut each potato in half lengthwise. Scoop out the insides with a spoon. Put the potato insides in a bowl. Set the empty skins aside.

3

(3) Put the cheese, butter, milk, and onion in the bowl with the potato. Add salt and pepper to taste. Mix with a fork until smooth. Put one-fourth of the potato mixture in each of the potato skins.

4

(4) Set the potatoes on a baking sheet. Bake for 10 minutes, or until the tops are golden brown. Sprinkle the chopped green onions over the potatoes.

FANTASTIC
Onion Fingerlings

You'll never be able to eat just one!

24

INGREDIENTS

2 pounds
fingerling potatoes

3 tablespoons
vegetable oil

1 envelope
onion soup mix

salt and pepper

TOOLS

cutting board

sharp knife

measuring spoons

large mixing bowl

pasta server

baking sheet

spatula

oven mitts

1. Preheat the oven to 450 **degrees**. Cut the potatoes in half lengthwise

2. Put the potatoes, oil, and onion soup mix in a large bowl. Mix until the potatoes are evenly coated. Add salt and pepper to taste.

3. Arrange the potatoes on a baking sheet. Bake for 20 minutes. Turn the potatoes over with a spatula. Bake for 20 more minutes.

1

2

3

SAVORY
Potato-Bacon Salad

A creamy dish ideal for picnics, potlucks, and parties!

INGREDIENTS

2½ pounds
red potatoes

1 cup sour cream

½ cup mayonnaise

½ bunch green
onions, chopped

1 cup grated
cheddar cheese

1 tablespoon
real bacon bits

TOOLS

large pot

pot holders

fork

strainer

large mixing bowl

spoon

cutting board

sharp knife

measuring cups

measuring spoons

mixing spoon

(1) Place the whole potatoes in a pot of water. Bring it to a boil. Boil the potatoes for 10 minutes, or until you can poke a fork into them easily. Drain the water and set the potatoes aside. Let the potatoes cool completely.

(2) Put the sour cream, mayonnaise, half of the chopped onions, half of the cheese, and half of the bacon bits in a large bowl. Mix well.

(3) Cut the cooled potatoes into cubes.

(4) Gently stir the potatoes into the sour cream mixture. Be careful not to mash them! Sprinkle the remaining cheese, onions, and bacon bits over the salad.

2

3

4

CHEDDAR
Potato Cakes

These cakes are corny, cheesy, and delicious!

MAKES 8 SMALL CAKES

INGREDIENTS

3 yellow potatoes, peeled

2 tablespoons butter

¼ cup milk

salt and pepper

½ teaspoon thyme

½ cup shredded
cheddar cheese

½ cup canned corn, drained

1 egg

½ teaspoon sugar

olive oil

TOOLS

cutting board

sharp knife

fork

medium pot

strainer

pot holders

measuring cups & spoons

mixing spoon

paper towels

peeler

can opener

plate

non-stick frying pan

spatula

1

① Fill a medium pot with water. Add a dash of salt. Bring it to a boil. While it is heating, chop the potatoes into 1-inch (2.5 cm) cubes. Add the potatoes to the boiling water. Cook for 10 to 15 minutes, or until potatoes are tender. Drain the water and return the potatoes to the pot.

② Add the butter, milk, and thyme. Add salt and pepper to taste. Mash thoroughly with a fork. Add the cheese, corn, egg, and sugar. Mix well.

③ Use your hands to form the mixture into eight round, flat cakes.

④ Put a paper towel on a plate. Heat ½ tablespoon oil in a non-stick frying pan over medium heat. Fry four potato cakes for about 5 minutes on each side. Put them on the plate. Put another ½ tablespoon of oil in the pan. Fry the other four cakes the same way. Serve warm.

2

3

4

WRAP IT UP!

Did you enjoy growing food from the earth? Are you a gifted cook with fresh ingredients? Fresh ingredients go a long way toward making food taste great. Ask the best chefs in the world. They'll tell you! Fresh ingredients are their secret ingredients!

By now you know that fresh food tastes great. Plus, it's good for the **environment**. Food from your garden doesn't require **transportation** or packaging. It isn't covered in harmful chemicals either!

So keep at it. Don't lose that green thumb! Think about your favorite foods. Can you grow them yourself? Chances are, you can. Check out the other books in this series. There may be a book about growing and cooking your favorite food!

Glossary

ALLERGY – sickness caused by touching, breathing, or eating certain things.

BLIGHT – a sickness that kills plants.

COMPOST – a mixture of natural materials, such as food scraps and lawn clippings, that can turn into fertilizer over time.

CONTAINER – something that other things can be put into.

DAMAGE – to cause harm or hurt to someone or something.

DEGREE – the unit used to measure temperature.

EMERGENCY – a sudden, unexpected, dangerous situation that requires immediate attention.

ENVIRONMENT – nature and everything in it, such as the land, sea, and air.

FERTILIZER – something used to make plants grow better in soil.

GARNISH – to decorate with small amounts of food.

MATURE – to finish growing or developing.

PINCH – the amount you can hold between your thumb and one finger.

SCRUB – to clean by rubbing hard.

SOLUBLE – able to dissolve in liquid.

TRANSPORTATION – the act of moving people and things.

WATERLOGGED – completely full of water.

Web Sites

To learn more about growing and cooking food, visit ABDO Publishing Company on the World Wide Web at **www.abdopublishing.com**. Web sites about creative ways for kids to grow and cook food are featured on our Book Links page. These links are routinely monitored and updated to provide the most current information available.

Index